BEHIND THE
SMILES

BEHIND THE
SMILES

An African Odyssey

Dr. Rilly Ray Rajkumar

PARTRIDGE

Print information available on the last page.

To order additional copies of this book, contact
Toll Free 800 101 2657 (Singapore)
Toll Free 1 800 81 7340 (Malaysia)
orders.singapore@partridgepublishing.com

www.partridgepublishing.com/singapore

CONTENTS

FOREWORD

Kitue is a town in Kenya, 180 kilometres east of Nairobi, around three hours by car. It is one of the poorest districts in the country. The climate is extremely hot. There is little rain, and the land is desert-like. Kitui has a population of around 155,900, making it the twelfth largest urban centre in Kenya. A large majority of residents belong to the Kamba, a Bantu people. The Kamba of Kenya speak Kikamba, their mother tongue, which is the Bantu Kamba language. The people are friendly and welcoming, especially to visitors. When I asked Bishop Anthony Muheria if he would like to have a visiting doctor for a few weeks, he gladly jumped at the chance. When I told him that she was an experienced specialist in primary care, he was even more enthusiastic.

The people here are poor, and healthcare services are few and far between. A female doctor from Singapore would not be just a novelty; she would work and bring much-needed medical care to the people.

Arrangements were made for Dr Rilly to spend some time at the local Muthale Hospital, to which the doctor's parish in Singapore, St Ignatius, had donated much-needed bed sheets. She would also spend time at a clinic in an even more rural parish. The plan was challenging. Dr Rilly experienced a type of medical practice very different from that which she had experienced in her own country. She interacted with the people and saw at first hand what true underdevelopment means.

The impact that one person can make is difficult to quantify, yet all doctors everywhere, at some stage of their lives, should try to do something similar to what Dr Rilly did.

The maternal mortality rate in the developing world is 1 in 17,000, while that of the developed world is 1 in 7. This part of Africa belongs to the developing world. There is just no comparison! There is so much to be done. If you would care to help in any way, with your time, your expertise, or a monetary contribution, we would be happy to hear from you. This book is the result of Dr Rilly's experiences among us; it is a worthwhile read to all who are interested in her African adventure.

If you are interested, you may contact me, Rev. Father Conor Donnelley, at frconor@googlemail.com

—Rev. Dr Fr Conor Donnelly,
Chaplain of Kianda Girl's School in Nairobi

Rev. Dr Father Conor Donnelly

Rev. Father Conor Donnelley belongs to the Opus Dei order of the Catholic Church. He is very committed to helping to improve the lives of the poor in Kenya.

The diocese of Kitui is one of the poorest in Kenya. Dr Rilly came here and spent a few weeks serving as a medical doctor in many of our dispensaries and at a hospital. She gave of her expertise and experience to the poorest of the poor; it had quite an impact. I was very grateful for her presence and her continuing goodwill and help.

I would like to use this occasion to encourage other medical personnel all over the world to consider following her example. I was pleased to be asked to write the foreword for this book, which recounts her experiences in helping the people of Kitui and of Kenya as a whole. I hope her story inspires many more to do the same.

We look forward to the input of medical minds in our efforts to improve health services in our communities. May God bless this book and all those whom it may inspire.

—Rev. Bishop Anthony Muheria
Bishop of Kitui

Bishop Anthony Muheria
Bishop of Kitui

Acknowledgements

S pecial thanks to Rev. Dr Fr Conor Donnelley, Chaplain of Eastland College of Technology and the Kianda School; Rev. Bishop Anthony Muheria, Bishop of Kitui; Mr Moses Muthaka, Marketing Manager at the Eastland College of Technology and Entrepreneurship Manager at the Informal Sector of Business Institute (ISBI); Ms Gabriella Tan, an IT Professional with excellent computer skills; Mr David Kraal, an experienced retired newspaper editor who offered me his advice; Ms Ruby Gomez, who provided IT advice; Ms Connie Lai of TIA Printers, who printed the proof copies; Ms Wendy Louis, a friend and experienced writer who edited the text; partially and Partridge Publishing, which published the book finally.

INTRODUCTION

What a joy it is to see the beautiful smiling faces of these children in red (cover picture). Seeing the camera, they rushed to pose for the photo. Their smiling faces mask the pain of hunger, poverty, and sorrow they experience in their homes. In Kenya, according to a World Bank document, four in ten Kenyans live below the poverty line, earning less than a dollar a day. It is different in my country, Singapore, where children are well taken care of by their families, the government ensures proper healthcare from the womb to the tomb, and compulsory education for all children is mandated by law.

The objective of this book is to help readers appreciate the extent of the pain and suffering of the poor in Kenya in order to motivate readers to help in any way possible, whether by volunteering their skills, experience, and expertise in education or construction or by donating money, materials, and service.

Despite their pain and suffering, their generosity to visitors is most admirable. While I was working in the hospital, they would smile and say good morning in their Kikamba language whenever I walked along the roads and pathways. I realized that this courtesy may have been extended to me because I was a stranger who looked different and dressed differently than they did. I confirmed that the other staff working in the hospital did not receive similar well wishes.

When we were driving to the hospital, the sister in charge asked me, "Doctor, what can we cook for you? What drinks would you like us to give you? I shall stock up the refrigerator in your cottage with the drinks you like and the fruits that you would like to eat." I was touched, and my answer was "I will eat whatever you eat; you need not worry about that." They did everything possible to make me comfortable. They are very hospitable to visitors.

At the hospital, I was given a tiny one-room cottage with all the basic amenities for comfortable living. One difference was that I slept under a mosquito net, spread out like a skirt from a ceiling hook. Its sides covered my bed and had to be tucked in on all the sides to prevent mosquitoes from entering and feasting on my blood. I really had to prevent mosquito bites in order to ensure that I did not get malaria, which is endemic in Nairobi and all of sub-Saharan Africa.

My cottage was on the same grounds as that of the three nuns who worked and lived there. They offered me their meals of local cuisine. They were tasty. Their hospitality and their culture – their dress, music, and dance – were beautiful and unique, and I loved them all.

The practice of their Catholic faith was important to them, so we had daily morning mass and prayers, after which we went out for our respective duties. They sang in harmonious soprano and alto voices with accompanying drums, as there were no musical instruments like the piano or the guitar. The school children would dance with rhythmic steps to the music as they went up for holy communion during mass. That was a great novelty for me. No prior practice was necessary, as they all already knew the steps, which were very repetitive. What a joyful worship that was for me!

Despite their rich culture, generations of poverty has taken a toll on the lives of the African people. It has reached such a complex state that to change things would require generations of astute planning and a multi-pronged approach to the development of all aspects of the people's livelihoods. Can a sustained, strong political will and an engaged community with international support that works together with law enforcement to protect the rights of the destitute turn the tide for these millions living in poverty? I believe the answer is yes. But it will require strong political will, determination, and commitment for generations.

After my first trip to Nairobi in 2008, the faces of the poor, especially the sunken faces of a woman I'll call Lisa and her babies (about whom I write in chapter 3), flashed across my mind so often that I had to go back two years later. But this time I went to serve the poor as a volunteer medical doctor in a village hospital in Kenya. In order to do this, I had to secure the approval of the Kenyan Medical Department, which took a year to process.

CHAPTER 1

KENYA, THE BEAUTIFUL AND THE UGLY

Gannet found in the coastal areas near Mombasa in Kenya
Picture from pixabay

Deers found in the wild animal parks

A road in a rich area of the country, that is well maintained

Lush vegetation and a stream seen in wet areas, arid, desert like terrain in dry area seen during the dry seson.

Map of Africa showing the location of Kenya.

Kenya, located in the east of Africa, is flanked by Ethiopia to the north, Somalia and the Indian Ocean to the east, Uganda to the west, and Tanzania to the south. It is touted as an idyllic destination for visitors.

The tourists see the beauty of Africa, while the volunteers see the poverty. The tourist brochures proclaim the breathtaking beauty of the exquisite flora and fauna, sunsets, waterfalls, mountains, and lakes. Other featured attractions include the Great Rift Valley, fruits, beaches, and springs. The brochures do not say much about the poverty there.

After their visits, tourists return with glorious pictures in their minds, which they advertise to their friends, thus promoting tourism, a source of revenue for the country. That is important, of course.

Kenya is most famous for its wildlife. With more than forty national parks and game reserves, you can view animals in the wild and go on a never-to-be-forgotten safari offering lifetime memories. Yes, Kenya is beautiful, but few get to see the underlying poverty and suffering of its thousands upon thousands of poor.

Half of the country's forty-three million people live below the poverty line and are unable to meet their daily nutritional requirements. When you meet these Kenyans, they are almost always smiling widely, but behind these smiles is a standard of living that is sustained on less than one Singapore dollar a day. More than three quarters of the population live in rural areas and rely on agriculture for their livelihood. About 70 per cent live in the central and western regions, which are devoid of reliable access to the necessary, basic human needs of healthcare, clean water, and sanitation. They also live without adequate food and other services required for the sustenance of the families.[1]

Agriculture is the mainstay of the African economy, the chief crops being coffee, corn, maize, rice, millet, and cassava. The mining of metals and precious stones also forms a large part of the economy. Kenya's gross domestic product (GDP) in 2013 was US$72.4 trillion. The challenges in this huge continent of forty-seven countries are many, but the principle challenge is how to reduce poverty, the root of all the misery.[2]

Infectious diseases are the main cause of death, even though most are treatable. This is because there is a shortage of medical and paramedical workers in Kenya, as they leave the country for better paying jobs. Consequently, services have been provided with inadequately skilled staff. The lack of piped water, modern sanitation, medicines, and equipment has been a stumbling block to the diagnosis and treatment of the sick. The effort is only complicated by poor infrastructure and a systemic lack of communication and transportation. There is seldom easy access to medical care, as communication is possible only by visiting on foot.

Most inhabitants of poor villages must walk for miles carrying their sick babies on their backs to reach a healthcare facility. Table 1 provides figures that will give you an idea of the healthcare situation in Kenya.

Table 1 Data from the Ministry of Public Health and the Ministry of Health and Sanitation of Kenya for 2013[3]

Life expectancy at birth	60 years
Annual deaths (per 1,000 persons)	10.6
Infant mortality rate (per 1,000 live births)	52
Neonatal mortality rate (per 1,000 live births)	31
Mortality rates for children under five years of age (per 100 persons)	74
Maternal mortality (per 100,000 births)	488
Adult mortality (per 100,000 persons)	358
Population estimate	39,476,794

Fifty-six percent of Kenyan women deliver their babies at home with the help of a birth attendant, with home births being more common in the rural areas. Maternal mortality and morbidity is the result of the interplay of socioeconomic states; cultural, economic, and logistic barriers; inadequate healthcare facilities; and underfunded preventive services, like immunization of mothers and babies. Low education levels and income factors also contribute to the situation. It is a well-known fact that in order to ensure the overall national health, a nation must focus on and provide for the healthy growth of children from the antenatal period, as well as enable them to grow up in good health so they can contribute positively to the nation's economy. In the long term, a sickly mother and child would be an additional burden on the healthcare expenditure of the country.[4]

In Singapore, by comparison, we are very fortunate. In 2013, our maternal mortality rate was 0 per 1,000 live births, and the infant mortality rate was 2 per 100,000 live births.[5] Singapore has one of the leading healthcare programmes in the world.

CHAPTER 2

POVERTY IN RURAL KENYA

Kibera and Mukuru are the poorest slums in Kenya. Kibera is five kilometres west of Nairobi, the capital of Kenya. This slum developed more than fifty years ago, during the British Colonial era, when the poor were pushed out into the barren outskirts while the rich occupied the city centre with all its modern amenities.[6]

The inhabitants of Kibera live on less than a dollar a day. Fifty percent of these residents suffer from HIV/AIDS, many of whom have very short life spans. Other common diseases include malaria, dysentery, and tuberculosis. Malnutrition among children causes stunted growth. About five hundred thousand to one million people live here in overcrowded and unhealthy conditions. Large areas are filled with garbage, soot, dust, and human waste. Fires often break out, due to the overcrowding.

Situated just outside Nairobi, the thirty-five-year-old Mukuru slum is home to nearly six hundred thousand people. Most families here are squatters, crammed into shacks measuring ten feet by ten feet. For many of them, the little they once had was taken from them when the owners of the land on which they previously resided evicted them. Being homeless, they end up here. Most of the people here are unemployed, except for a few who are labourers in nearby factories. Some earn paltry sums from selling a few eggs from their scrawny chickens and milk from the one or two goats they own. Most children here do not go to school. Just to survive, many resort to prostitution, begging, and crime. Child labour is also common. Many children become orphans when their parents die from illnesses, mainly HIV/AIDS.

Slum shacks on either side of the railway track
that runs from Nairobi to Mombasa.

The rubbish heaps in this slum stretch out on either side of the railway line and are growing faster and taller than the children.

Another view of the railway track,
shelters, and rubbish heaps.

The government and some international agencies have jointly embarked on a project to make some upgrades in the slums, but the challenges are so many that some estimate that the project may take up to ten years or more to complete.

CHAPTER 3

FIVE CHILDREN BY DIFFERENT MEN

We met Lisa (not her real name) in Mukuru. She had five children, all by different men. She does not remember which man was the father of which child. We met the man who was Lisa's last partner. He helped her when she was ill after the second-to-last child was born. He provided food for the family in return for sleeping with her. Lisa became pregnant with the last two babies within a year of each other. Her oldest girl was married as a teenager and stays with her husband. The second girl was sickly and was sent to a children's home. Lisa could not bear to see the third and the fourth children die slowly, wasting away in her presence, so she tied them up on the railway track, hoping the train would run over them and kill them instantly. A neighbour, seeing this, took the children away from the track to her home. She adopted one and sent the other to an orphanage. Lisa decided to nurse the youngest, but sadly, the baby died of HIV/AIDS after only a few months. Lisa also died of HIV/AIDS soon after.

When we first met Lisa in 2008, and her face was very different. She was healthy and happy. We saw her again after three years, and she looked very different then. It is difficult to believe they show the same woman. After three years, Lisa had lost a lot of weight. The life had gone from her face, and only pain and misery showed. Note the sunken cheeks and prominent collar bones, both signs of poor nutrition. The man in the picture was her last partner; he soon disappeared, leaving her to cope alone with the children This is a common story here. The man seems happy – probably a sign of his satisfaction with what he gets from her!

Young women here have no opportunity to be educated. They typically get married very early, give birth to many children, and then suffer trying to take care of them. Domestic violence is common; the unemployed men resort to alcohol and crime. Many women become single mothers after their partners leave them other woman or die from illness, commonly HIV/AIDS. Eventually, when the mother dies, the children become orphans who roam the streets, as we see in the picture below.

Little children wandering aimlessly without any adult
supervision. The adult here is the author.

Together with his team of youth leaders, Rev. Dr Father Conor Donnelly, a medical doctor and a priest of the Opus Dei order of the Catholic Church, gathers these street children in order to counsel them, talk to them, and engage them in group activities to enhance their healthy growth and correct their attitudes. Those who can study are sent to school. Funds come from the Catholic Church in Nairobi. The team also attends to the needs of the families in the slums, providing them with food, clothing, and assistance.

Some of the youth leaders have graduated from secondary schools and others from Strathmore University, a private university. Motivated by the needs of the community, they have committed themselves to helping other young people who are in need of guidance to better their education. Some of the leaders provide hands-on support, while others mentor the children, educate them, and give them lessons and talks to encourage them to study and work hard so that they may prosper in life. These youth leaders are an impressive group of young men with admirable values, seen in the way they carry themselves and speak.

Rev. Dr Father Conor and his team of youth leaders.

Chapter 4

Life in the Slums

Most homes in the slums are zinc-roofed sheds with broken walls, allowing rainwater seepage. Overcrowding is common, with people and animals, like goats and cattle, living under the same roof.

A cluster of shelters with goats outside and rubbish in front of the doorway.

Due to the lack of modern sanitation, pit toilets have been constructed by volunteer groups, but they are now worn out, due to age. Residents who are far away from them often defecate in plastic bags and throw them onto the rubbish dump in the middle of the slum next to the railway track. The area is named "Flying Toilet".

In a May 2014 meeting of the UN about the Millennium Development Goals, the assistant secretary general, Jan Eliasson, commented, "I am moved by the fact that every two and a half minutes, a child dies from preventable diarrheal diseases linked to defecation. These are silent deaths – not reported in the media, not a subject of public debate. Let's not remain silent any longer."

A billion people have no choice but to defecate outside onto the ground in full view of other people. So to address this situation, the UN renewed its efforts to drive progress in sanitation and water. At the meeting, there was a strong commitment by the member states to end the practice of open defecation in underdeveloped countries by 2025.

Pit toilets, with broken windows, leaking roofs, and doors that do not lock. Privacy is of no importance here. The "lucky" ones get to use these toilets, while the others use "flying toilets".

An area of rubbish dumps and "flying toilets". Note the
tall factory in the background owned by a rich tycoon,
where the children are employed as child labourers.

Education of Children

Most children do not go to school for various reasons, poverty being
the primary one. Child labour is rampant, and it is often the only source
of income families have to meet their daily needs. Working long hours, the
children are so tired that they are unable to study. Moreover, most parents
have very limited budgets and are unable to buy textbooks and writing
materials for those few who can go to school. Unless there is some drastic
intervention, the majority of these children will grow up poor and remain
poor, thus continuing the poverty cycle, perhaps for generations.

A classroom in the Mukuru slum. Note the holes in the classroom walls, which allow rainwater seepage. The wooden desks are worn out with cracks and rough surfaces that have not been not replaced for years.

A crowd of children crammed into a classroom.

CHAPTER 5

FUN FOR THE SLUM CHILDREN: A RARE EVENT

A Singapore volunteer group of three visited the slum area. They planned to give the deprived children a sumptuous meal and a handful of sweets and to fix a net in an assigned area for a makeshift basketball court. A member of this group cut the pink ribbon stretched across the poles for the opening ceremony. It was an occasion of great joy seldom experienced here.

Schoolboys playing in a makeshift basketball court.
The great thrill of shooting the ball into the net was a novelty.
The opening was marked by a member of our group cutting
a ribbon, after which the thrilling game started.

Schoolgirls at the only school in the slums lining
up to collect sweets from Singapore.

Slum children waiting for their first a chicken-drumstick
lunch. What a gustatory joy to look forward to!

The joy of tasting a chicken drumstick and a
desert of ice cream for the first time.

A cluster of shelters above and one below donated
by the Church of St Ignatius in Singapore. Note the huge
factory at the back owned by a rich businessman

This is the shelter donated by St Ignatius church in Singapore. Moses Muthaka is standing in front of the shelter. He is the team leader of Rev Fr Conor's team of helpers.

The Church of St Ignatius of Singapore also donated, bedding, blankets, toys, teddy bears, clothes, surgical equipment, medicines, and an ambulance for the hospital.

Another shelter named Mathew.

Chapter 6

Muthale Mission Hospital

It was a different experience working as a full-time doctor in a village hospital – Muthale Mission Hospital (MMH), situated in a town called Muthale. It serves about 500,000 people. Situated in the Catholic Diocese of Kitui, it's run by the Catholic Church. Bishop Anthony Muheria, the bishop of Kitui, and his team of staff administer this hospital and the two satellite clinics located in remote parts of the diocese, where there are no other healthcare facilities, no piped water or sanitation, no electricity, and no proper roads. The clinics work by candlelight during the night shifts.[7]

Muthale is located in the district of Kitui, one of the poorest districts in Kenya. This north-eastern part of Nairobi suffers from drought almost all year round. The drought causes water shortages and poor harvests, resulting in hunger for families and farm animals. These long periods of drought often cause the families here to fall into an unimaginably severe level of poverty.

MMH is run by a board of management headed by the Bishop of Kitui, and members come from both religious and secular organizations. The seventy-six-bed hospital was founded in 1948 by the religious congregation of the Franciscan Missionaries of Africa. The institution was upgraded to hospital status ten years later, and the management was handed over to the Little Sisters of St Francis. It now offers the following services:

- inpatient, outpatient, and emergency medical, surgical, and obstetric care
- caesarean sections
- minor surgery
- growth monitoring and promotion for children
- family planning
- immunization
- HIV/AIDS diagnosis, treatment, monitoring, and prevention
- home-based care and health education
- management of childhood illnesses
- prevention of mother-to-child transmission of HIV
- support services – including pharmacy, laboratory, X-ray, and ultrasound services – run by a few paramedics.

A notice outside the office of the Catholic Diocese of Kitui.

During my visit, there were two MBBS graduate doctors at the hospital, including myself, and a team of paramedical doctors, nurses, laboratory technicians, support staff, and ambulance drivers. Facilities were very basic and inadequate. The staff, however, are very hard working.

In Kavisuni and Liani, the two satellite clinics of MMH, basic primary care services are provided by a team of trained paramedics, who work as doctors and nurses.

Women seeking healthcare walk for miles, barefoot, with their ill babies on their backs, as public transport is not available.

In the picture below, an ill child with a fever is being examined. The mother walked for miles with her baby on her back, as shown. The baby was diagnosed with malaria, which is endemic in this region and is commonly seen both in adults and children. Whereas in Singapore we treat malaria only after a blood sample taken from the patient comes back positive for the malarial parasite, in Kitui, diagnosis is based purely on clinical symptoms and signs. The condition is so common that clinical diagnosis is correct most of the time. A laboratory diagnosis would require laboratory equipment and technicians, which are unaffordable here.

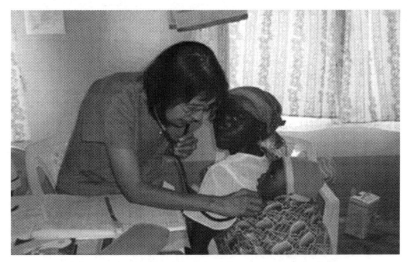

The author examining a sick mother and child
in a hospital outpatient clinic.

Malaria, although treatable, is the leading cause of morbidity and mortality in Kenya. It is estimated that malaria is responsible 20 per cent of all deaths among children below the age of five years, about 40 to 70 per cent of all outpatient visits, and 20 per cent of hospital admissions. The most vulnerable groups are children and pregnant women.

The government of Kenya has developed a ten-year strategy for malaria management (2009–2019) called the Kenya National Malaria Strategy (KNMS). It's goal is to reduce morbidity and mortality caused by malaria. Its four areas of focus are

- care management,
- vector control,
- epidemic preparedness and response, and
- monitoring and evaluation.

Malaria infects around 200 million people a year and killed an estimated 584,000 people in 2013, most of them in sub- Saharan Africa.

In July 2015, Europe's drug regulators recommended that shots of Mosquirix, a new vaccine that the WHO had approved for use against Malaria, be given for Malaria prevention in Africa. The drug is produced by GlaxoSmithKline, a drug company in the United Kingdom. This program is partially funded by the Bill and Melinda Gates Foundation. So there is hope.

Seven million children die each year in Kenya, mainly from preventable and treatable conditions. These children could be saved through interventions, including childhood immunizations, the administration of antibiotics for pneumonia, oral rehydration therapy for diarrhoea, and the provision of insecticide for malaria prevention.

In Kenya, one third of the children are stunted (too short for their age), a sign of chronic malnutrition related to poverty. Poverty is also responsible for the higher childhood mortality rates in rural areas. Kenya is ranked thirty-ninth globally and has the highest death rate in children, under the age of five and suffering from malaria.[8]

Women and their babies in a maternal and children's
heath clinic at MMH. A nurse checks the temperature of the babies prior
to seeing the doctor. Only a small group of children are able to
attend these clinics, and the treatment default rate is high due to
limited accessibility and other various economic factors.

Chapter 7

The Boy in a Coma

I was on night duty, which my African counterpart, Dr Mark, and I took turns covering. I was fast asleep when the nurse called me at one o'clock saying, "Doctor, you are on duty today. Please come instantly to the male ward to see and treat a young man in coma. Come quickly!"

My heart started beating fast. I jumped out of bed, thinking, What could that diagnosis be? A young man in coma? A series of possible causes went through my mind as I rushed to the ward.

The boy was nineteen years old. He was totally unconscious in bed with a host of relatives around him looking very anxious and speaking in their language, which was strange to me. The ward nurse translated for me.

"The family was having dinner when the boy said he felt feverish, after which he felt very giddy and slumped down in his chair. The father caught him. He was limp. He mumbled a few strange words and soon was unable to talk. Then he became unconscious. They quickly drove him in a relative's car to the hospital."

I examined him. He was in a deep coma, unresponsive to all clinical tests. I conferred with the chief nurse as to what it could be. He said confidently, "This is a case of cerebral malaria. We see these cases here every day."

He is experienced, and he must be right, I thought. I still needed to confirm with Dr Mark, the other resident doctor, who was asleep. I felt hesitant to wake him up but had no choice in this situation. He confirmed the diagnosis, and we immediately administered the cheapest drug effective against malaria. An intravenous drip was put up with the medicine, quinine, in it. This drip continued throughout the night.

I went back to my room, but the question of whether this boy would be alive the next day weighed heavily on me. I could not sleep and lay praying that he would not die under my care. I stayed awake, waiting patiently for the morning so that I could check to see how he was doing in the ward. To my great surprise, I saw him standing at the entrance of the ward, waiting to go home. I gave a sigh of relief. That was a great miracle for me.

On returning to my cottage certain thoughts occupied my mind. For this young man, the outcome was joyful, but what would have been the psychological effects on the surviving family members if he had died; this is indeed the outcome of malaria morbidity for a large number of Kenyans. In a poverty-stricken community where death is an almost daily occurrence they accept it as a normal event. Their daily struggles to meet the basic needs of food, water, and shelter wear them out, so they have no time to think about why it happened and what was the real cause of the death, and whether it could have been prevented. There is an unrelenting anxiety about how they will get food for their families' for the next meal. In these circumstances, the situation does not improve, as people are not in the position to make demands.

CHAPTER 8

THE ELOPING GIRL

She was a fifteen-year-old girl who had completed secondary school. The mother had paid for her studies in a college so that she could earn a decent living. She was running away with her boyfriend on a motorcycle from Muthale to the big city of Mombasa. When her mother heard about this, she sent a friend to follow them by car and bring her daughter back, which the friend did.

The girl was so angry at being brought back home that she swallowed almost the entire contents of a bottle of detergent that night. She became unconscious and was brought to Kavisuni Clinic for treatment. She was treated appropriately and had recovered by the evening, after a whole day in hospital. She went home but refused to continue her studies. Sadly, she ended up as a teenage mum with many children, living in poverty. This is a common story among the young women from poor families.

This teenager would have been influenced by her boyfriend to go to Mombasa, a place with international tourists, fun, pleasure, and the bright lights. The realization comes too late that the glitter and glitz is only temporary. Some get so enamoured with city life that they seek more and more fun and entertainment. Besides draining their finances, the pursuit poisons young minds with sloth, alcohol addiction, drugs, and sex and dulls their moral values.

What caused this girl to leave her family and elope with her boyfriend to Mombasa? Was it the grinding poverty, poor parenting, or loss of societal moral norms? We do not know. Perhaps it was all of these.

CHAPTER 9

THE ELDERLY
MAN AND THE INFANT

B rought to MMH by his son in a friend's van, the man was seventy-
five years old, frail, and weak. He was paralyzed on his left side and
could not speak, due to a stroke. We transferred him onto a wheelchair and
brought him into the ward. Like many others, he was unaware that he had
high blood pressure and uncontrolled diabetes mellitus. He was diagnosed
too late when the illness brought him to the hospital. We examined him
and put him on an intravenous drip to treat his dehydration, as he could
not eat or drink. He succumbed to his illness and died the next day. His
illness was too advanced, with a very high blood glucose level that could
not be brought under control.

The average life expectancy in Kenya is fifty-six years. The main
challenge comes from communicable diseases (CDs), such as those caused by
infectious agents like malaria and HIV. The increase of non-communicable
diseases (NCDs) like diabetes and hypertension has added to the challenges
Kenya already faces. There has been an increase in incidences of all the three
categories of diabetes: Type I, Type II, and the gestational diabetes seen in
pregnant women.

The double demands now made on the healthcare system by CDs and
the rising trend of NCDs has hindered Kenya's progress towards achieving
the Millennium Development Goals. Due to the lack of resources allocated
in these areas, there has been little progress in implementing cost-effective
strategies for disease prevention, treatment, and control.

Unlike the treatment of CDs or infectious diseases, where antibiotics achieve good results, NCDs require a multi-pronged approach to achieve results. The effective prevention and treatment of diabetes, for instance, requires early diagnosis, adequate treatment, health education, and long-term lifestyle changes, like receiving adequate nutrition, exercising, controlling weight, quitting smoking, and not being sedentary. In Kenya, a disproportionate amount of money is allocated to the urban areas for curative care, and only a relatively meagre sum is allocated for diabetic care. But allocating resources for effective programs, health promotion, and health education has been known to reduce the burden of healthcare costs over the long term.

The following day, I saw an infant of eight months brought by a poor, worried mum. The baby was wheezing loudly and gasping for breath, and the mum was very anxious. It was very painful to see. Oxygen was administered through a mask, but there was no equipment to monitor the oxygen saturation and vital signs like heart rate, respiratory rate, and body temperature. In Singapore, we monitor these things instantly. The babies recover quickly because the monitoring equipment enables us to administer the required treatments. This baby died after five hours in the hospital. The facilities were inadequate, and the baby was too ill to go to the city hospital, which was a good five hours' drive away. The baby would have died on the way.

What made watching that child gasp for air and ultimately die right before my eyes doubly painful was the helplessness I felt. I felt so useless, as I could do nothing else to save the poor child. This would never have happened in my country, where we are so fortunate to have all up-to-date, modern emergency facilities. In the Singapore children's hospital, the very ill babies are admitted and treated in the Intensive Care Unit (ICU) of the hospital. They all survive.

It was all emotionally devastating. I felt like a useless doctor who could only stay with the sad mother with my arm on her shoulders. No words would comfort her. The great hope with which she had come to us was soon shattered when the baby exhaled her last breath. The mum screamed, tears pouring from her eyes, saying words in her language I could not understand. My tears fell too as I felt despair, hopelessness, and helplessness.

Not all babies are brought up in families with medical and social problems. The picture above shows a stable and a happy family. This mum is aware of the need to visit the hospital for the routine immunization of her babies against the illnesses that can cause death in children below the age of five years – diseases like diphtheria, tetanus, pertussis, hepatitis, measles, mumps, and rubella. Unlike the majority of women here, she is also aware that babies need to come to the hospital for prompt treatment when they are ill. The father works in the village administrative office. The mother cares for the home and family, and he brings the money for the family's expenses.

CHAPTER 10

HIV/AIDS IN KENYA

Kenya has among the the highest incidences of HIV/AIDS in the world. In a 2010 United Nations report on the country, it was estimated that 1.5 million people were living with HIV/AIDS. In that year, 1.2 million Kenyan children were orphaned and 80,000 Kenyans died from HIV/AIDS-related ailments. The prevalence among women was 8 per cent and was 4.3 per cent among men.

With present awareness, education, treatment, and prevention programs for HIV/AIDS, there has been a decline of 6.35 per cent per year. The home-care program is carried out by a group of trained volunteers who provide counselling, follow-up, and education for patients and families. MMH has implemented the treatment recommended by the World Health Organization, and the medications provided to the patients are jointly financed by the government and volunteer organizations.

All drugs for the treatment, including the expensive retroviral drugs, are made available to the patients free of charge. Sadly, the default rate of the attending patients is high due to lack of transportation, illnesses, poverty, poor education, and lack of understanding of the need for regular follow-up and treatment. As a result, mortality and morbidity among adults and children are still high. In a previous study conducted in a Kenyan hospital, it was found that 10 per cent of the mothers who delivered were HIV positive. It was estimated that the rate of HIV/AIDS in the population was about 7.5 per cent.[9] About one million children are orphaned due to HIV.AIDS.

A group of HIV/AIDS patients waiting to see the doctor with the administrator of Muthale Mission Hospital, Sister Consolata Katua. The smiling faces mask the reality of their pain and suffering from the debilitating illness of HIV/AIDS. Do they know what can happen to them in future, and did they tell their younger family members how to prevent HIV/AIDS?

One doctor in that hospital was trained was trained in the treatment of HIV/AIDS and manages all patients coming for treatment. She was able to treat one patient who has been stable on retroviral drugs for twenty years and is now holding a full-time job. This lady is one of the few very motivated ladies in the community

CHAPTER 11

THE CATHOLIC CHURCH IN KENYA

The Catholic Church in Kenya has played a major role in the development of medical and social services and in the livelihood of the poor in Africa. It's historical development and growth in Kenya is shown in the following timeline: [10]

- 1498 – Vasco Da Gama erects a cross on the in the seashore of Malindi in Kenya on his way east to spread the faith.
- 1542 – St Francis Xavier visited Malindi on his way to Goa.
- 1543 – A community of six hundred Kenyan Christians established themselves in Mombasa.
- 1599 – Augustinian Fathers arrived in Kenya to evangelize.
- 1860 – French Holy Ghost Fathers arrived with Fr Tom Burke
- 1902– Consolata Fathers arrived
- 1903 – Mill Hill Fathers arrived

A century ago the Mill Hill Fathers established St Augustine's Mission in Nairobi. Subsequently, the faith spread to other parts of Kenya.

The Missionary Society of St Patrick was set up in 1951 in Nairobi by the Irish fathers. Then, at Rome's request, dioceses were established in Kenya in the provinces of Lodwar, Eldoret, Nakuru, and later Kitui.

The Roman Catholic Diocese of Kitui is situated 112 miles east of Nairobi and covers two administrative districts, Kitui and Muingi. Out of a population of about one million, 15 per cent are baptized Catholics. They are served by twenty-three parishes, each about seven miles apart. Gradually, the diocese grew, adding more priests and more baptized Catholics.

The Church in the district of Kitui is headed by Bishop Anthony Muheria, a young, well-educated, dynamic, and spirit-filled leader who works hard to improve the lives of the poor. He has a hard-working team to support him.

From the left: Bishop Anthony Muheria, bishop of the diocese of Kitui; Sister Consolata Katua, administrator of MMH; and Sister Margaret Wanda, who helps to supervise and run the health programs in MMH and the two satellite clinics under the Kitui diocese.

CHAPTER 12

WEATHER IN KENYA

Kitui lies south of the equator close to the Sahara desert. It's an area which is prone to long periods of severe drought. Lodwar, the province in the north-west of Kenya, is dry all the year round, whereas Kitui in the south-west usually has short spells of rain in October and May.

In 2009, Kenya experienced a severe drought and famine, and the death toll rose to thousands of people and animals. In the rural areas, where agriculture is the mainstay of the economy, the severe drought resulted in very poor harvests, resulting in poor income and therefore severe conditions for the people.

The pain and suffering these families experience from poor nutrition and the lack of clean drinking water exacts a heavy toll on their health, resulting in early death, especially in young children and the elderly. The Kamba people, who inhabit this area, grow only subsistence crops like corn, beans, peas, yams, millet, pumpkins, oranges, lemons, grapes, and so on. They also rear animals like cattle, goats, and sheep. The prolonged dry spells push farmers to the brink of starvation, as food prices soar and cattle raids spiral out of control. The implementation of drought alleviation projects focuses on temporary and inadequate interventions with no long term plans. This is partly due to inadequate budgetary allocation and a lack of planning for proper intervention during times of drought.

There have been some projects to address the drought situation. The Red Cross national societies of Kenya, Norway, and Finland are working together on a project both to bore holes for water to irrigate the fields and to build pipes to carry that water to the villages. In 2012, the government started a multi-billion-Kenyan-shillings irrigation project in the town of Muingi, as well as an irrigation project costing 3 billion Kenyan shillings in the town of Usueni. The people here can look forward to a brighter future.[11]

In January 2014, the government of Kenya warned of an impending drought that would affect an estimated 1.6 million people in the north-eastern, north-western, and south-eastern parts of Kenya. It has had an impact on households, cattle, and agriculture. The situation has become worse with the increasing food prices. During this period, families face the death of their children, the elderly, and those affected by illness. The situation has only deepened their dire poverty. On dry and parched land, due to drought, there are dried up trees and burnt crops, and died from hunger and thirst.. carcasses of dead animals, that

CHAPTER 13

THE SHE-GOAT PROJECT

Agriculture is one of the principal means of livelihood for the majority of the people of Africa. Besides growing various crops, rearing animals has been a mainstay of the economy. The urban farms owned by rich merchants have gradually enlarged and prospered, producing large crop yields and rearing increasing numbers of animals. Business has progressed and reached international levels of trade and industry. The rural areas have been slow to pick on this mainly due to the continuing poverty of the rural villagers and families.

The She-Goat Project, which started in Kenya in 2013, is slowly picking up in some of the poor villages in the rural areas. Since the project is small and easily managed, it has been possible for poor families to adopt and enhance this project to enable them to improve their livelihoods. Muanga district in Kenya has adopted the She-Goat project in a small way. Villagers are given female goats to rear. They are told how to take care of the goats, feeding, housing, and caring for them, and then they are given some information on when to mate them with a neighbour's male goat. When a female baby is born, it is donated to the next poor farmer, who is encouraged to continue with the same care and to encourage breeding.

The Catholic Church, with the help of Fr Conor and his chief helper, Moses, has donated sixteen goats to the poor families in this village. Other parishes in that area were told to identify poor families, so that the eleven female baby goats born to the first group could be given to them. This system was initiated in Gitugu village in 2013. The men, who were idle before, are now enthusiastically working on this. Their families benefit from the milk and the dung, which is used to fertilize their gardens so that they produce rich crops.

One woman with five children was given a goat and a cow to feed her children. She is now able to sell some milk from the cow and the goat. This allowed here to get a loan from the bank to enhance her business. Stories like hers are most heartening and touching to hear. These people are truly grateful for this help.

Initially the farmers are taught the various skills of goat care – housing, feeding, and health and disease prevention – as well as marketing. They promise that the first female baby goats will be donated to other poor families in the village. Families are able to grow their business and focus on its future. There are many weekend markets where goats are bought and sold by merchants. It is interesting to see a busy market on such a day. The air is filled with the noise of bargaining and the odour of animals.

Many voluntary organizations have taken up this project, focussing on its growth by giving the families start-up finances, skills, education, and assistance in managing the teething issues and helping them move towards future independence. Some families have worked hard on this and have gained larger incomes, thus getting out of poverty.

When they were told that their photos would be taken, they went in to dress up with their Sunday best in order to pose for the photos to look their best

This is Edith (not her real name) given to her family to feed her babies and if possible sell some milk to make some money Their real names are kept confidential.

This is Charley (not his real name) where the goat is pregnant and he has promised to give the babies to other poor families in the community to propagate the goat project to help the other poor families.

This is Maria (not her real name) who is proudly
posing with her animal gift to help propagate the goat project
in the village, and work hard to make it a success.
They dressed in their Sunday best to take these photos.

CHAPTER 14

THE BEAUTY OF KENYA

The pain and suffering of the destitute is one aspect of life in Kenya. The other aspect, in contrast, is the unusual charm of the animals and landscape. They do not see the suffering of the poor. Africa can boast of its natural resources, massive land area, animals, flowers, vegetation, and precious stones; the beauty of all these has a unique allure.

Kenya is endowed with an abundance of fascinating things to see. It is a land of natural beauty, renowned for its rustic ambience, ancient history, and the unique cultural gifts of the music, dances, and costumes of the people. If you decide to volunteer to work with the poor, you may want to also unwind and relax on the beautiful beaches, one of the loveliest being Diani Beach. There are multiple activities offered for visitors there, and the view is breathtaking.

Mahali Mzuri is an authentic luxury camp with zebras, hippopotamuses, leopards, cheetahs, wildebeests, and elephants all wandering in the vast, natural landscape. Masai Mara is a well-known safari destination. Lamu Island has unique rock formations. There are also dormant volcanic mountains. Then there is the well-known Mount Kenya and Kapsowar, a pretty town in the Rift Valley. There are the Lihuru Gardens and Meru National Park. Finally there is Giraffe Manor, a luxury accommodation where Rothschild Giraffes are seen wandering around. That is most fascinating.

In the hot season, the major roads are lined with beautiful red bougainvillea and the bright-yellow flowering cassia trees. Travelling along the city roads is a beautiful experience.

The beautiful bougainvillea flowers over the fence of a home.

The bright-yellow cassia adorning the trees outside
the Kitui secretariat of the church.

A tree full of mangoes seen in the wet season

Fruits like mango, banana, jackfruit, and passion fruit grow plentifully in the wet season. We saw the trees heavily laden with fruits in the villages we passed on the way to the village hospital.

Mother Nature has given Africa beautiful birds, too, as well as many species of monkeys. I encountered a majestic crowned crane, a family's pet that freely roams in their home garden. He pecked my sandwiches from my plate when I was looking away, talking to a friend. His long neck was an advantage, for sure. Isn't he beautiful! He was so beautiful that I could not get angry with him but just kept admiring him and his graceful walk in the garden.

The pet crowned crane.

Giraffe the unique native of Africa

Leopard

Beautiful duck

Parrots in love

Mum and baby

Diamonds and Other Gemstones from Africa

Kenya has many mines producing diamonds and other precious stones. Foreign companies engage in the extraction of these gems using native labourers. The companies, along with the local elite, enrich themselves while the mine workers are poorly paid, work in dreadful conditions, and remain poor.

Kenya, like some other parts of Africa, is well known for its gemstone mining. Small-scale miners dominate the industry. The government is trying to further develop the industry, which is responsible for 60 percent of annual gemstone output in the world. One of the well-known companies producing and marketing these precious metals and precious stones is Swensson and Simonet Minerals Kenya, which has its office in the Nairobi municipality. There are a few other multinational companies, too, who benefit from the trade.

Unfortunately, the wealth generated from this industry does not benefit the mine workers, and the poor. While the men and women in rich communities adorn themselves with these gemstones, the miners remain desperately poor.

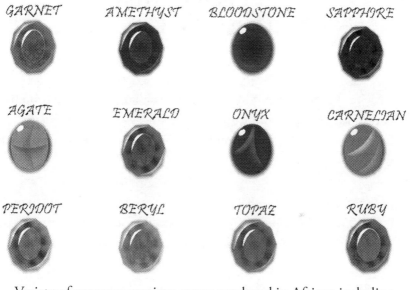

GARNET AMETHYST BLOODSTONE SAPPHIRE

AGATE EMERALD ONYX CARNELIAN

PERIDOT BERYL TOPAZ RUBY

Variety of gorgeous precious stones produced in African including
in the Kenyan mines. They make elaborate and very expensive
jewellery, imported tothe rich countries in the world.

CHAPTER 15

THE PEOPLE AND CULTURE OF KENYA

Kenya has become culturally diverse as a result of migration from north and south of Africa and from Arabian and European countries.

The country has forty different ethnic African groups who speak a variety of languages.

The languages spoken in Kenya fall into three groups: Bantu languages, spoken by 60 per cent of people in sub-Saharan Africa; Cushitic languages; and English. In Kenya, the most widely spoken language is Swahili – Bantu infused with Arabic. Kenya is home to a large population of Europeans, Indians, and Pakistanis who have migrated to the country since the nineteenth century and who primarily speak English.

Kenyans learn African music and dancing from a young age. One of the most popular forms of pop music is called Benga, a traditional African drum and dance with an attractive rhythmic style that is very enjoyable to witness. In cultural gatherings, children and adults join in the dancing without having to learn the steps. Even during the Catholic celebration of the Mass, children go up for communion dancing to the beat of the drums with natural rhythmic steps that they all seem to know well. That was a novelty for me to see, and it was beautiful. The only music used was the drum. There were no pianos or guitars.

Music and dancing constitute an important part of African culture. From very young the children learn the steps from the adults and sway their bodies beautifully, which beautiful to experience. There are no piano or violin or any other musical instrument that accompany the dances. The drum beats are the only equipment commonly used.

Women dancing and singing
accompanied by rhythmic drum beats

Kenyan women have a unique style of dress involving long skirts, blouses that reach below the waist, and remarkable head dress, which are coloured pieces of cloth wrapped round the head in an elaborate style. One of our friends attempted to dress as an African woman, though not as elaborate in style.

African women in their national dress dancing at a wedding

A tribal woman in their national jewellery round her neck

School children dancing in a school celebration event. They learn the steps from young so that they may be able to dance even when they are older as part of their national culture.

School girls praying before they start dancing in school

In the remote villages there are indigenous tribes. who may be identified with their dressings and jewellery they wear round their necks and ears. The practice of witchcrafts happen during festivals, marriage celebrations and illnesses invoking the spirits.

Across the cities and other villages in Kenya, two thirds of the people are Christian. Arabic traders settled in the country, so some Kenyans became Muslims. Though the majority of people are Christian and Muslim, however, many still believe strongly in the ancestor world where the dead have power for good and bad over their living descendants. Many religious rituals are influenced by these beliefs.

CHAPTER 16

THE ROCK CHURCHES OF LALIBELA: THREE-THOUSAND-YEAR-OLD MARVELS

One cannot fail to mention the ancient rock churches still standing in Lalibela, 645 km north of Addis Ababa, the capital of Kenya's northern neighbour, Ethiopia. Lalibela stands in a mountainous terrain 2,400 meters above sea level. A single, huge mountain rock was cut piece by piece to build these amazing rock churches. They used the most primitive equipment. The prevailing myth says that these wonders were built by the angels in the twelfth and thirteenth centuries.

Tradition says that King Lalibela (1185–1225) of the Zagwe Dynasty had these churches "sculpted" after a dream in which he was told by God to build them. The king is said to have had the help of the angels, who worked during the nights while the workmen worked during the day.

After a pilgrimage to Jerusalem, the king was so inspired by the Holy City that he created a second Jerusalem for his people in Africa, because he realized that few of his people could make the long and expensive pilgrimage to Jerusalem.[12]

A large wooden screw was used by the craftsmen to bore
into the rock when they built the ancient churches.

An ancient tool box holding construction equipment
for the building of the rock churches.

The rock churches are clustered into two major groups, one representing
the earthly Jerusalem and the other the heavenly Jerusalem. A deep trench
between them is supposed to represent the River Jordan separating them.

Alleys between the churches provide pathways to walk from one side to
the other. These pathways are deep, rough, rugged surfaces that are slippery,
undulating, and difficult to traverse. One needs to be very careful walking
on these pathways to ensure one does not slip and fall.

A deep valley lies between the two groups of rock churches,
and the pathway is rough, with cobbled surfaces.

St George's Church (Biet George). Its roof is constructed in the shape of a
Greek cross. It has twelve sides with windows and doors. It is four-storeys
high and has twelve gates bearing the names of the twelve tribes of the
sons of Israel. Tradition has it that St George himself visited this church
during its construction, leaving the footprints of his horse on the rock.

Inside, there are markings concerning the prophecy of the New Jerusalem, which is referred to as the Heavenly Jerusalem in the book of Revelation and as Zion in other books of the Bible. In Christian tradition, the New Jerusalem is a city that will be established in south of the Temple Mount and will be inhabited by the twelve tribes of Israel. Justice, holiness, and righteousness will characterize this reign, and the guilty will be condemned. Jesus will then rule with the power of the Holy Spirit in what is called the Messianic era.

A clear view of the cross-shaped roof of St George's Church. Steps lead down four floors to the entrance of the church. In the foreground is Andrew Sunil Rajkumar. The rock churches have been declared world heritage sites by UNESCO. Some of the parts that are weak and weather-beaten have been renovated by UNESCO in order to maintain the site's original beauty

View of another church.

The priests in white are of the Ethiopian Orthodox Christian faith,
which worships the Old Testament. They sit at the entrance for light to
read their scriptures in the Aramaic language, the language of Jesus.

Some of the documents of the Aramaic Bible were first seen in 701 BC. A few more were documented in 500 BC, followed by still others in the third century AD. As time progressed, more and more documents were researched and studied by scholars. Theological studies focused on the Hebrew Bible scripted in the Hebrew language, as we see in the text below.

A page from an Aramaic Bible. It is a language that few understand.

The villagers, dressed in white, sit on the ground
in front of the churches to pray

Processions of Orthodox priests take place during special celebrations, like Christmas and Easter. Community members gather in large numbers for these occasions. For Sunday prayers, too, the community gathers, all dressed in white with white headdresses. They sit and kneel on the ground while the priests chant prayers inside the churches. The prayers are amplified through the use of a microphone. The congregation is quiet and reverent. Nobody uses books; they know the prayer responses by heart. This is a wonderful scene for me because I have not seen this level of piety anywhere else.

A priest carrying two crosses, representing the two different churches in Lalibela. Behind him are frescoes, which use colours made from the dyes of ancient plants that have maintained their brightness. The art of producing and using the natural dyes for painting is most amazing. The paintings commemorating ancient rites, done 3000 years ago, have maintained their bright colours for centuries – a marvel indeed.

Chapter 17

Reflections

Living in poverty is painful and beyond the imagination of most of us – no home, no clothing, and no food. There are several definitions of poverty, but perhaps the most appropriate is "a phenomenon where families have been impoverished for at least three generations." People often cannot break out of this economic state, and so it is frequently referred to as the poverty cycle.[13]

Of all the poor living in the underdeveloped world, the largest number live in Africa. It has been said that the amount of wealth and food in the world would be enough to feed and house all the people if shared equitably, but this is hardly the case in reality. Human greed and dulled consciences are so prevalent in us that even when we have enough, we strive for more with an insatiable appetite. The thrill of getting more is so exciting that, quite unconsciously, our consciences get dulled and unethical practices take root. Excess food, for example, gets thrown away, clothes get moth eaten, and silverware turns black. Human greed, corruption, and the fight for power have been rampant in our countries for centuries. When it spreads, that greed, the cancer of the soul, is difficult to curb or cure.

The example of Singapore, which has grown from an underdeveloped country into one of the world's advanced economies in the last fifty years, is commendable. I believe curbing corruption through the strict implementation of laws was the key factor in this progress. Besides this, laws to strengthen security, free healthcare, education for all children, and compulsory childhood immunization programs were the building blocks of development. Healthcare programmes against diphtheria and measles, universal availability of immunization for newborn babies, and the strict enforcement of these laws were the keys to progress. Anyone, irrespective of status, engaging in corrupt practices was dealt with severely through imprisonment, large fines, and finally, loss of his or her job. Such individuals were also featured in the news along with their photos as a deterrent. Accountability for expenditures and truthful accounting are mandatory by law for all government departments, private organizations, and banks, and the records are subject to strict, regular audits.

But one could argue that Singapore is tiny compared with Kenya. Nevertheless, the essence of these policies could be adopted and tailored to suit each country according to its needs. There is a saying that goes "if there is a will, there is a way forward". The will needs to exist in the nation's political system. Africa enjoys substantial contributions from foreign organizations and NGOs year after year, and yet the resulting reduction in poverty is paltry and not commensurate with the large amount of funds donated. In many areas in Africa, transparency, competency, and accountability are wanting. One billion children in poor countries in the world go to bed hungry, the largest percentage of them in Africa.

Various international organizations have been involved with projects to achieve poverty reduction in Africa, including the following:

- European Commission
- Food and Agricultural Organization
- Global Environmental Facility
- International Finance Cooperation
- Organization of Petroleum Exporting Countries
- Global Fund
- United Nations Development Program in HIV/AIDS
- United Nations Fund for Population Activities
- United Nations Industrial Development Organization
- World Bank
- World Food Program

Many other organizations from the Netherlands, Japan, Sweden, Belgium, and Germany also give support for poverty reduction in Africa.[14]

In addition, there have been smaller innovative programs, like Heifer International, a non-profit organization first started in 1944 by Dan West that now based in Little Rock, Arkansas, USA. This organization works to reduce poverty by donating animals, like cows, goats, water buffalo, pigs, llamas, frogs, rabbits, and bees, and by providing training in agricultural methods. Its aim is to develop self-sufficiency and growth in communities. The first three cows the organization donated were named Faith, Hope, and Charity'.[15]

The recipients of these animal babies had to promise to give the first female offspring of their animals, as well as pass on the skills and knowledge of animal husbandry and agriculture, to another poverty-stricken family. This program has been successful and sustainable in 125 countries from 1944 to the present. In 2008, the Bill and Melinda Gates International Foundation awarded the organization a $42.5 million grant to help poor, rural farmers in East Africa to double their incomes. Did this result in poverty reduction? We do not know.

Another striking project is the Graduation Program, which is another holistic program that uses the strategy of giving poor families cows or other animals and training them to raise them. It also provides months of food and cash support to help families not to have to sell the animal for food when in a financial crisis. In addition, it provides education on micro-savings, health education, and regular coaching to reinforce skills and build confidence. This program had been successful in India, Ghana, and Pakistan, even three years after it started. Whether it has been extended to Africa, we do not know.[16]

The Solar Sister program empowers women to use solar energy to provide light for study and home activities and in the process to save costs and improve well-being. It has been successful in the most remote communities in rural Africa. Women learn the science of clean technology and recruit other women to the project with the aim of spreading it to other parts of the country. Currently the program is growing slowly, but the growth has surely been achieved by motivated and enterprising women.

Could the slow growth be due to little support it receives from the men in the communities?[17]

The other concern being researched at present is the influence of human emotions related to poverty. It is likely that individuals who experience a state of poverty where physical health has been poor from lack of food and the basic minimum amenities for living are likely to lose hope. After all, the human mental state is influenced by the physical, social, psychological, and spiritual elements, and these are interrelated. A state of poverty can result in a loss of hope and self-esteem if there is no help on the horizon. The resulting lethargy can sustain the poverty cycle through generations to come.

A study is on the way to determine whether the power of hope can break the poverty cycle. On the other hand, could hopelessness and stress create a "poverty trap" in which people surrender to a whirlpool of despair? Some economists and psychologists are finding evidence to support that fact. More research is on the way to find evidence to support this.

In a document published recently by Pope Francis titled "Care of Our Common Home", he addressed the tragic effects of environmental degradation, which affects the lives of the world's poorest. He identified the positive suggestions made by some that are being drowned out by the indifference of others, resulting in slow progress. We require a new responsiveness and universal solidarity, as everyone's talents, wills, and strong efforts are needed to redress the damage caused by poverty in order to rectify it for the benefit of all humanity. We live in a common home, our world. Mother Nature is already rebelling with the extremes of droughts, floods, tsunamis, and earthquakes. We need to wake up to take quick action, or else we will suffer the consequences. And the poorest among us will be affected most.[18]

In 2014, a meeting of African leaders was held in Washington DC. This Committee was chaired by Mr Kofi Anan, the previous secretary general of the United Nations. The African leaders discussed ways to achieve poverty reduction. They highlighted the dire state of poverty in Africa and the ways the continent was losing funds for the development of the country. It was demonstrated that the present ways of doing business were unethical, and as a result, the continent was losing out on income for its development.

There was rampant tax evasion, no transparency in business dealings, no accountability, and a lack of ethical business practices. The leaders concluded that fair and ethical business investments are the key to Africa's economic transformation.[19]

In a conference held in July 2015 in Kenya with business leaders, US president Barack Obama emphasized the fact that the major area to address is rampant corruption. Only after doing so will Africa prosper, and this, in turn, will bring greater equality and reduce poverty.

Can this poverty cycle in Africa be broken? I believe it can if there is a strong political will to reduce poverty and an equally strong commitment to do so on a long-term basis, even for generations to come. Transformation can happen. It took the United States a few generations to begin improving its level of poverty. Addressing what was termed the "War on Poverty" in his 1964 State of the Union address, then president of United States Lyndon B. Johnson called on congress to pass a law called the Economic Opportunity Act. The law, which passed, set aside federal funds to target poverty. That was the beginning. It's not that poverty has since disappeared, but this was a starting point. While the laws need to be strictly enforced, food, health, and education are the catalysts for change.[20]

Although we live outside Africa, the world is our home – our Mother Earth – and poverty is a global challenge. We have a responsibility to help Africa's poor by sharing, in our little ways, our skills, time, and funds by volunteering our resources.

The words of Mother Teresa come to mind. She said, "The most terrible poverty is loneliness and the feeling of being unloved. The biggest disease today's not leprosy or tuberculosis, but rather the feeling of being unwanted."

We think sometimes that poverty is only being hungry, naked, and homeless. But being unwanted, unloved, and uncared for is the greatest poverty; we must start in our own homes to remedy this kind of poverty.

"At the end of our lives, we will not be judged by how many diplomas we have received, how much money we have made, or how many great things we have done. We will be judged by 'I was hungry and you gave me food. I was naked and you clothed me. I was homeless and you took me in.'"

—Mother Teresa

Appendix

HIV AIDS Treatment

Foll here (Ref 11) WHO
- *Revised antiretroviral therapy in children*
- *National recommendation*
- *AIDS Control*
- *Use of ARVs for mothers in labour and delivery units*
- *diagrammatic circle for use if possible ref (8) WHO*

References

1 Kenya home rural poverty portal:www.ruralpovertyportal.org www.google.com.sg/webhp?source=search n.d

2 [PDF]Kenya Health Policy 2014- 2030. Ministry of Health Republic of Kenya "Towards attaining the highest standard of health" published by the Ministry of Health, Afia Home Cathedral Road, PO Box 30016, Nairobi 00100 By James W. Macharia, Cabinet Secretary, Ministry of Health: http://afidep.org/wptb_dl= 80

3 Africa Development Indicators 2012-2013, Latest issue 2012-2013, Washington DC, June 27, 2013, www.worldbank.org/en/region/afr/publication/africa- development indicators-2012-2013

4 Maternal and Child Health report 2013, Kenya. www.who.int/pmnch/media/membernews/2011/20121216_kenyaparliament.pdf. paper by Inter-parliamentary Union - Inter- parliamentaire, 2013

5 Maternal and child care report 2014 by same organization as above

6

*6. 1 Kibera Slum: http//www.google.com.sg/webhp/ source=sear4ch. app+gfe...http://en.Wikipedia.org/wiki/Kibera_slum, 2012 2/5/2016 n.d

*6.2 Mukuru Slum. http//en/wikipedia.org/wiki/Mukuru_slum 2012, n.d

7 Muthale Mission Hospital. mutyhalehospital.org http//www.dioceseofkitui.org, n.d

8 Malaria in Kenya- Fact Sheet. KEMRI (Kenya Medical Research Institute)www.Kemri.org/index.php/...a...fri may 06, 2016

9 USAID Kenya HIV/AIDS/Agency for Ijternational Devepoment.http://www.usaidgov/news=information/fact.../usaid-kenya-hivaids, n.d

10 A belief History of the Catholic Church in Kenya, http://www.facebook. com/ Holy Catholic Church, Kenya.../ 488565767893, n.d

11 UNDP Millenium Development Goals, progress reports, Africa www. undp.org/content/undp/en/home.library page/mdg/mdg/report/africa-collection-htm/contents, report 2016, 5/4/2016 (date access)

12
    *12 Lalibela:A Guide to Lalibela, Araba Books, book published in Ethiopia. 2008
    *12 Lalibela. Wikipedia, the free encyclopedia, http://en.wikikipedia. otg/wiki/Lalibela

13 Cycle of Poverty=Wikipedia, the free encyclopedia. http://wikipedia. org/wiki/cycle_of_poverty

14 United Nations National, Human Developmental Reports. http:// hdriundp.org/en/2013 report 9/5/1016 (date access)

15 Dan West and Heifer Project. Dan West (philanthropist).www.heifer. org Wikipedia the free encyclopaedia. http://en.wikipedia.org/wiki/Dan West(philanthropist) n.d

16 Graduation Project Creating Pathways out of Extreme Poverty into Sustainable Livelihood apr 2013: www.worldbank.org/en/results/ 2013/04/04
    Sustainable Livelihood for the Reduction of extreme Poverty. International Conference. "Graduation and Social Projection" Serene Hotel, 6-8 May, Kigali, Rwanda. graduation@fund-action.capital.org

17
    17.1 Solar Sister: Eradicating Energy Property through Social Enterprise. http://solarsister/org. n.d
    17.2 Also Solar Energy "Rays of Hope "Solar Energy Empowerment, "Waisini Island" Power of the Sun": http://www.youtube/ube.com/ watch?v= WEV2tDgXFtk

18 Pope Francis: Laudate Si 23/5/2015. w2.vatican.va/...francisco/papa-francisco 20150524_enciclica

19 Africa Program Panel, Fair and Ethical Investment are the key to Africa's transformation 2015. Conference with President Obama, Washington DC

20 War on Poverty. Wikipedia - the free Encyclopaedia: http://en.wikipedia. órg/wiki/war_on_poverty/ n.d

Printed in the United States
By Bookmasters